Racing Against The Shadow Of Alzheimer And Dementia

The Complete 2023 Care Giving And Support Guide.

Milton Tucker

Credits

Table Of Content

INTRODUCTION

The purpose of this book is to focus on practical solutions that will support the person with the illness, as well as caregivers, family members, and friends, in empowering the skills, talents, and abilities that remain as the disease develops.

There is guidance for persons at different stages of Alzheimer's disease or related dementia. Learn to enhance your unique powers and talents as the disease advances. There are also ideas for caretakers, family members, and friends to assist them grasp.

What is physically happening in the brain of an Alzheimer's patient? Caregivers and family members may utilize this information. Members and friends may enable persons with Alzheimer's disease to express their dreams and accomplish their goals.

Each chapter opens with a scenario in which a girl and her father go out to eat supper. These scenarios are meant to help carers understand the changes that could occur as the disease advances. The reader gets a firsthand glimpse at what life is like for the caregiver and the person for whom he or she is caring.

Following these instances is an outline of the specific sickness stage and a description of how the disease affects the brain.

General caregiver guidance is followed by specialized ideas to aid the person with Alzheimer's disease in adjusting and dealing with the changes that are occurring. These tips come from caregivers and other professionals who care for persons with Alzheimer's disease or related dementia every day. The guidelines offer caretakers ways to focus on the skills that remain in the face of prospective losses in critical brain functions.

I propose that you read through the full book to get a feel of how the condition advances, and then go back and concentrate on how to execute the recommendations stated for the stage in which you find yourself living and working. Consider how you may make each stage as fruitful as feasible for the person suffering from the ailment. Because every human is given unique talents, skills, and abilities that may be demonstrated throughout life; hunt for chances to increase those residual advantages.

This guide For Alzheimer's Condition arranges the material in a manner that adds to the empowerment of the skills and talents of individuals living with the condition as well as their caregivers, family members, and friends.

CHAPTER 1

Old Age Symptoms Or Is It Time To Treat Alzheimer?

We may sometimes suffer a decline in one or more of the critical brain processes during our lifetimes. We forget somebody's name or are briefly unable to express ourselves. As we discover, things that used to be simple for us now take longer. These losses may sometimes be brought on by stress, insufficient sleep, or physical.

It is only reasonable to question if a persistent decline in the brain's essential capabilities a symptom of aging or whether it may be an indication that the brain is growing ill. Most individuals express their worry by asking, "How can I know whether I am developing Alzheimer's disease or another dementia?" Or they question, "Do I already have Alzheimer's disease or another associated dementia in its early stages?"

Often referred to as "benign senile forgetfulness," the normal changes of aging in the brain are anything but "benign" since they may make people very anxious. And the worry itself may make these symptoms worse.

What changes may one anticipate as their brain ages?

Some of them are easy (and are just memory lapses). Forgetting someone's name, especially if you haven't seen them in a long while. Having trouble coming up with the correct phrase to describe oneself or even forgetting the name of an item, event, or another thing, especially if it is something you are not quite acquainted with.

One unfavourable effect of these alterations is that sometimes the person seems to require urging to remember the correct words. Things also slow down as we age, which means that: It takes longer to pick up new knowledge or abilities (particularly complicated skills or ideas). Reaction times are slower (reflexes take longer, and overall processing is slower).

But one aspect of the regular aging process is that general intelligence, sometimes known as "psychomotor functioning" or "cognitive functioning," stays normal and that judgment and reasoning skills are unaffected.

Alzheimer's disease symptoms are really far more troubling than merely a little memory loss, and they start to limit one's capacity to carry out daily tasks. For instance:

✳ difficulties doing routine chores and everyday activities, such as forgetting appointments, instructions, or other things like turning on the shower's water and then leaving it on.

✳ difficulty balancing a check book, leaving the water running; getting ready without taking a shower; and leaving the water running

✳ difficulty with meal preparation or cleaning; used to be able to balance.

✳ making strange choices or behaving improperly.

✳ difficulty learning new things—still going back to the same place rather than moving on to something new.

✳ dread of leaving familiar surroundings; suspicion of other people's intentions

✳ an excessive reliance

✳social disengagement, apathy, and passivity—loss of interest in friends or hobbies; propensity to sit about and do nothing

✳sleeping more than usual, watching television or looking into space, and conversing little or not at all.

These changes don't happen overnight; rather, they develop gradually over many months. There isn't one specific behaviour that can be used to diagnose or label Alzheimer's disease. However, a person who has several of these behavioural indicators suggest that the person is likely going through anything more than merely normal brain aging. Dementia, the medical name for the steady decline in intellectual capacity brought on by Alzheimer's disease, may very well be that something.

To ensure that a curable condition is not the source of the symptoms, a professional must do a thorough physical and neurological evaluation. Once all potentially curable disorders have been ruled out, it is probable that a brain issue is what is causing dementia. It may be a condition that is destroying nerve cells, such as Alzheimer's disease.

Alzheimer's Disease: What Is It?

The cerebral hemispheres of the brain experience the gradual loss of nerve cells as a result of the disease. Depending on the individual circumstances and health of each afflicted person, the disease's development might endure for anywhere between 8 and 20 years.

Despite certain similarities, each person with Alzheimer's disease or related dementia experiences the illness in a different way. The degradation does not happen in a step-by-step, regular manner since the illness develops at its own pace.

There is a time of denial for everyone who is suffering from the beginning of the illness, including the afflicted individual as well as professionals, carers, family members, and friends. Numerous tests are performed to rule out other potential causes of the behaviour changes in the patient with the suspected condition.

The sickness usually begins in a very subtle way. Only in hindsight can the family put the puzzle together and identify symptoms that the sickness had already begun.

For people who have Alzheimer's disease as well as for those who live and work with them, looking into the future may be terrifying. Even though the illness process may endure for many years, the individual generally passes away because of another condition that is occurring concurrently in the body, such as heart disease, cancer, or renal failure.

Although there are several stages during Alzheimer's disease, this book reduces the classification to only three: the Initial/Mild Stage, the Average Stage, and the Advanced Stage.

These divisions are comparable to characterizing the "stages" of a child's development and conduct, such as during the first year of life, the second year (the "terrible twos"), adolescence, etc. A person with Alzheimer's disease steadily loses abilities as the illness worsens.

Brain activity occurs, and in many respects, more childish behaviour starts to show. The goal of "staging" the sickness is to provide rules for formulating plans for ongoing care. This may retain the person's dignity and maximize their talents. Many talents are still in use even if there are losses as the illness progresses.

You may wish to read the parts of this book that pertain to your requirements right now since trying to comprehend all the changes that will take place throughout the 8–20-year period during which the illness advances can be difficult and even terrifying. The best course of action is to take each day as it comes and pay close attention to the needs of the person you are caring for.

CHAPTER 2

The Initial/Early Stage: Something Is Not Right

OUR LIVES ARE OVERFLOWING with hopes and aspirations. Some of those hopes and ambitions have come true. Others have not. Life is different than imagined for those who have Alzheimer's disease or a similar dementia, as well as for their carers, family members, and friends.

When caretakers keep in mind that Alzheimer's disease just affects a person's memory and not his intellect, respect and affection will remain throughout the progression of the condition.

✳ A woman conveys to her daughter who is providing care for her in the initial Stage her preferences for medical care throughout the long-term course of Alzheimer's disease.

✳ When people who have never painted before enrolling in Memories in the Making classes—an art initiative sponsored by local Alzheimer Association chapters—and produce the stunning artworks that enable them to communicate their feelings, respect and affection are shown in the Moderate Stage.

✳ In the Severe Stage, even though her father was unable to communicate his requests verbally, a caregiver nevertheless brought his bed outside into the patio every sunny day since they knew how much he liked being outside.

In all stages of the condition, every person with a diagnosis of Alzheimer's disease or a similar ailment is entitled to certain specific rights. Thinking about these rights may assist carers in adjusting their caring to respect the person's dignity as the illness progresses and preserve the abilities and capacities that are still there.

A Typical Scene

Alexander's Delight is a favorite restaurant of your father and you, therefore the two of you have made plans to lunch there. He turned 85 years old today. Your father greets you and remarks, "This is a wonderful location. Look at the wall-mounted plates and the decorations from the 1950s. This is something your mum would have enjoyed.

Dad, we've been here a hundred times before, you respond, shocked. Do you not recall? He replies, "No, we haven't. I'm doing this for the first time. You allow the topic of discussion to change. It's time to place your menu order. "I believe I'll have the chicken-fried steak," your father adds. Mom and both of you used to like that supper. What do you mean, asks your father? Meatballs and pasta are my go-to meal.

You add, "Dad, you said that you and Mom used to come here often and that you enjoyed chicken fried steak when we were here on your 82nd birthday." Your father starts to respond and quarrel. The meal was less enjoyable than when you were honoring his 82nd birthday. After the initial shock and worry have subsided and an Alzheimer's disease diagnosis has been established for your loved one, you will find yourself transitioning from being a temporary caregiver to realizing that your caring is now permanent. You may certainly find several signals that were there during the last few months or years that pointed to this day. The moment to learn as much as you can about the brain changes that will ultimately influence all of the critical abilities and talents that we sometimes take for granted when things are going well is now.

The moment has come to adopt a fresh perspective on Alzheimer's disease. While the losses you experience in your loved one may make you uneasy, you have a choice as to whether you want to dwell on these losses and maybe feel overwhelmed, or if you want to start looking for the good indicators of life and dignity that are still there.

You may choose to accept what is occurring and recognize that this is your life right now rather than hoping that it would go according to how you had always imagined it would. If you gradually alter your perspective on life's circumstances, letting go of certain things and embracing others, it may be just as gratifying. With this new perspective, we must consider our own self and the changes we must make to deal with the illness. Finding strategies to support the person with Alzheimer's disease in making up for their condition and feeling in control requires greater ingenuity from us.

It is simple to forget or fail to realize that people with Alzheimer's disease still have the ability to self-reflect and the desire to be contributing members of society because of the pervasive views about aging and dementia that present in modern culture.

Failure to alter our perspective on Alzheimer's disease puts our loved ones at danger of improper behavior or inadvertent harm. It is reassuring to keep in mind that not all essential brain processes will decline at the same time. Negative behaviors might creep into our caring approach when we overlook or fail to appreciate the other tasks.

When memory deteriorates, speak to people with Alzheimer's disease as if they were children or just ignore them. As language declines, laugh at their efforts to communicate or give up attempting to figure out what they want to say. When they are still able to do a challenging activity, do things for them or don't expect them to do them alone. **Avoid the following;**

✳ As their social skills deteriorate, be hesitant to bring them to family events. ✳ Be ashamed of their conduct when their judgment and logic are flawed. Avoid bringing them out in public since walking becomes difficult. ✳ As their senses are compromised, we neglect to create an aesthetically beautiful and engaging atmosphere because we don't believe they are capable of appreciating their surroundings.

When we search for the dignity in people with Alzheimer's disease, we seek for solutions to compensate for, deal with, and adapt to their constantly evolving lifestyle. We believe that despite the illness, the capacity for reflection will persist. Our new style of thinking will include finding solutions to enable people to continue being useful and valuable members of society. To assist children access their long-term memory when their short-term memory starts to wane, we might: Find photographs and ask them questions about what they recall about the images. Play activities with children, such as asking them to name items around the home to develop language and engage in native-language conversation with them whenever possible. Consider the skills they developed prior to the onset of the sickness and provide time for them to continue practicing them, such as painting, photography, gardening or other pastimes.

Early acquired skills that need sophisticated performance are often retained throughout the course of the illness. To maintain social contact, invite folks to call often, go on walks, or schedule regular visits to a nearby restaurant.

✳ Recognize that thinking and judgment are inconsistent, and that we will need to make choices to keep them safe. ✳ Play activities to get people moving while you find safe areas to walk or drive. ✳ Play some music, keep the holiday decorations up, or just arrange a good table to create a dynamic environment that will please the senses. Everyone wants to be treated with respect and decency.

Here are some instances of people who have the illness and their reflections on the illness itself:

✳ Alzheimer's patient clinical nurse: "I've lost my memory but not my mind. I can sometimes look at myself as a "patient" and observe what is occurring because of my line of work. ✳ "I used to handle numerous things," a businessman who once worked for a Fortune 500 firm said. Still, I want to contribute what I can. Please don't believe that by giving me envelopes to lick, I'll be satisfied. All of the family's clothing, including men's suits, caps, and such items, used to be handmade by a mother. When handed some needlepoint to do with her kid, the woman tested it out, glanced at the girl, and then flung the supplies on the ground out of disgust. ✳ Do I still have my mind?" a spouse questioned to his wife. For God to give me this, I must have been pretty awful in my life. This is not how my life is meant to be. ✳ I don't understand why they won't let me attend to church alone, a former university professor pondered. ✳ An Alzheimer's patient's wife observed: "Throughout our marriage, we told each other every day, 'I love you!'" Even when we were angry with one another, they were never just meaningless words. Today, we still do it, but it seems like we do it more often. In the past, I was often the one to start these daily declarations of love. Today, he initiates them more, and I take comfort in the knowledge that he still loves me actively and intentionally.

In the cerebral hemispheres of the brain, ALZHEIMER'S DISEASE CAUSES the gradual, cumulative loss of nerve cells. Every nerve cell in the brain performs a special function that only that nerve cell can accomplish, and no other nerve cell can, setting the brain apart from other bodily organs. Every component of the brain has a distinct purpose, and for the brain to function properly, all of the components must cooperate. Because no other portion of the brain can take over or carry out that function, losing any region of the brain also means losing that function.

The hippocampus, which is situated close to the middle of the cerebral hemispheres, is the first location in which nerve cells perish in Alzheimer's disease. The brain's hippocampus is where memories are stored. The hippocampus organizes and stores every memory. The remaining brain functions must be treasured and, with the help of the caregiver, presented more vividly, as Alzheimer's disease gradually destroys them.

Memory loss is the first sign of Alzheimer's disease in the Early-to-Mild stage. However, the remainder of the brain continues to function properly, allowing the individual to continue moving, feeling, seeing, hearing, and integrating information. Because judgment, logic, and social skills are still intact, the individual may build coping mechanisms to cope with the memory issues because these abilities are still intact.

Because of these compensatory measures, the individual will seem normal and never seek medical attention at this early stage of the illness process, making it likely that no one will be aware of the issue. As Alzheimer's disease advances, damage to the brain shifts from the hippocampus to the temporal lobe, making it difficult for the affected individual to comprehend words or use the appropriate words while speaking.

Conflicts with other people might result from difficulty understanding or utilizing language, and it can also make a person retreat and communicate less. The individual attempts to understand why other people don't appear to react to dialogue correctly since their frontal lobes are still functional.

During this initial stage, the emphasis should be on the talents, abilities, and skills that are still there and may be developed. Focus on developing the talents and abilities that are still there rather than fretting about losses. A caregiver for a person with Early Alzheimer's disease is a fight between wanting to help the person who has been diagnosed and questioning whether you should.

You may be wondering if it is preferable to let people be independent and take care of themselves (but sometimes in a different manner) rather than to step in and take care of them.

Caretakers will find it most beneficial to avoid doing activities for patients in the Early stage of Alzheimer's disease that they can accomplish for themselves and to promote independence as much as possible.

The caregiver's job is to serve as a resource and an advocate. Observe without intervening, unless there is a risk of abuse or bodily harm. Consider when it would be best for you to take the lead, when you should delegate authority, and when it would be ideal for the person with Alzheimer's disease to take the lead. In addition, **before** issues emerge, learn as much as you can about the condition. ✻ When you feel unwell, see your family doctor for a comprehensive physical as well as a geriatric assessment center or other medical institution that specializes in dementia or Alzheimer's disease. Dementia may be brought on by a variety of factors, and although it often cannot be cured, it can sometimes be assisted.

✻ Based on what the person with dementia is experiencing, try to comprehend and discuss the brain functions that are still there as well as those that have been lost.

✳ Any and every information you have should be shared with family members who are interested in learning more about the condition.

✳ To talk about life changes and evolving family pressures, call a family forum. Think about incorporating the dementia patient in this conversation. ✳ Be prepared for both your personal denial and the denial of your loved one and other family members that they are suffering from the sickness.

✳ Be honest when telling people that you, your partner, or a friend has Alzheimer's disease.

✳ Tell your emotions to a spiritual counselor. A counselor can assist in separating what is true and what is emotional.

✳ Consult your family, friends, and counselors at the local Alzheimer's Association branch. **Plan** for your long-term comfort and care if you are your own caregiver.

✳ Decide which members of your family, your friends, and other people can help you when you are responsible for handling all of life's responsibilities on your own.

✳ Be ready to assume the initiative in all everyday activities. For example, it's crucial to set up all financial legal paperwork while the person with Alzheimer's disease is still able to participate in the process. Learn about the resources offered by your local or national Alzheimer's Association branch. You can assist those you meet who could end up caring for someone with Alzheimer's disease or a similar dementia even if you just have a basic understanding of the subject.

✳ Be a proactive listener and pay attention to what the person you are caring for wants to say. He may wish to discuss delicate subjects like power of attorney or long-term care. He could wish to share with you something that worries him that he is aware of.

Keep in mind that the sickness will dictate the course of events. The person you are caring for may often not want to make plans for the future. Move ahead with these concerns at his speed rather than attempting to push this kind of conversation.

Additionally, your doctor could advise taking certain actions at times. When you can, adhere to them. What is my purpose in life? is a common question that people with Alzheimer's disease or caregivers ask. What should I do at this point? How can I go about living my life as effectively as possible?

For the caregiver, it is important to remember the patient's dignity and to always look for methods to respect that dignity.

Aid the individual in developing and maturing while she still has the ability to do so. Try to have the self-control to pause before acting or speaking and ask yourself, "What's going on here? Is the person I'm concerned about actually doing or saying these things on purpose?

It is important for the diseased individual to keep doing what they can for as long as they can. Find coping mechanisms that will aid with your memory of upcoming appointments, callers, and other aspects of everyday living. Everyone has losses throughout their lives, whether they are brought on by Alzheimer's disease or not.

The majority of caregivers for people with Alzheimer's disease are aware of the illness's first effects on short-term memory. The caregiver must keep in mind that people with Alzheimer's disease often are also aware of their memory loss. Find out what's actually vital as early in the illness process as you can.

Use the advice below to assist someone discover what she wants from life. Being able to tell what a person wants from what she really needs to be whole and accepting of that is a necessary part of maintaining dignity in your relationship. Habitual activities are still doable and might make a dementia patient feel productive.

Create memory cues by: Create lists, illustrate basic actions using images, and adhere to regular procedures. Because of their diminished short-term memory, they will need prompts and signals to know what to do.

✳ Keep extra sets of your vehicle and home keys. In case the person with Alzheimer's forgets where the keys are, locate a prominent spot to hang them so that they will be simple to discover. You must also reconsider if driving should be authorized at the same time.

✳ Make a note of where things are kept in the bathroom and kitchen. Label the 30 dressers, cabinets, and drawers. Utilize reminders like as calendars, pill boxes, and other tools. Positively word your inquiries and directives. Be aware that the individual might feel upset with his growing reliance on others and is typically conscious of a loss of abilities.

It might be difficult for her to adequately convey her feelings with words. Continue to be a resource and assist the individual in expressing themselves as a caregiver. Enjoy the comedy if the Alzheimer's patient finds it amusing when she can't find the right term and can laugh with the caregiver when it is eventually discovered. If appropriate, fill in a name or term that is lacking to save the individual from becoming irritated. Trainer and cue:

✳ Prepare the environment for encounters with the dementia patient. Try taking a polite, calm, and objective stance. Your laid-back attitude can spread.

✳ Before you start talking, make sure the individual is paying attention to you by looking straight into her eyes. Wait a few minutes and try again if you can't grab the person's attention the first time.

✳ Speak in uplifting phrases. Don't provide too many directives and try to avoid being too strict with your instructions.

✳ Don't complete sentences for those who have dementia. They could feel embarrassed by this. Allow them some time to express themselves and find the right words, but if and when that doesn't happen, gently suggest what they may want to say.

✳ Speak slowly, using different words or short sentences, and repeating yourself if necessary. Ask for feedback and watch for it in your facial expressions and body language.

✳ When speaking slowly and in brief phrases, try to avoid speaking in an arrogant tone of voice since this might make people angry. Being patient while speaking in this way is challenging. Remember that respectful communication shows consideration for others and upholds their dignity. A genuine apology, though, will demonstrate your respect if you've "lost it."

✳ Ask straightforward questions with a "yes" or "no" option as opposed to open-ended inquiries. You may ask, "Do you want to wear this green shirt or this red one?" in place of, "What would you want to wear today?" or "You look great in this outfit, why don't you wear it today?" Keep him informed by saying things like, "This is what you'll wear tomorrow," since the individual may still be interested in the choice of clothes long after they are unable to choose their own. You may also say, "This will be the ideal clothing for what we're doing tomorrow."

✳ When speaking to someone who has Alzheimer's disease in a group, don't treat them as if they don't exist. Don't react on the patient's behalf; let him speak. This is particularly crucial at medical appointments, when you must assist him preserve dignity by refusing to respond on his behalf.

✳ Share your emotions openly with those who have Alzheimer's disease. It communicates to them your continued need for them and your respect for their viewpoints.

✳ By expressing your emotions, you may relax and provide comfort for the other person. This is very significant. When you have been really irate and agitated and "lost it" with him.

✳ Be upbeat, hopeful, and comforting to the individual. Use phrases like "Everything will be OK" while speaking. "Stop worrying," We are doing well. "We're going to finish this." I am here to assist you.

✳ Don't try to stop the individual from discussing difficult and sensitive topics like death. Don't discount or reject sensations by saying, "That won't happen," for example.

✳ Instead of calling the individual with Alzheimer's disease "he" or "she," use their actual name. Prior to Alzheimer's disease, tasks completed repeatedly and often tend to be maintained the longest. Consider the following advice as well. Organize circumstances for success.

Recognize how long a person with Alzheimer's disease can focus on a task. Before the tension gets unbearable, watch for signals that irritation is starting to set in and redirect his attention.

✳ When a person with Alzheimer's disease is having difficulty getting dressed or putting on his shoes, do not hurry to assist.

✳Setting the table, putting 33 clothes back in the closet, and other straightforward tasks. If given the opportunity to continue working on the assignment, he will often complete it.

You shouldn't step in unless he requests your assistance. Recognize that a work may not be completed as meticulously as it would have been before to the start of Alzheimer's disease.

✳ Be careful not to delegate responsibility to the individual by saying something like, "Here! No, you can't. Provide it to me. Focus on what the individual can accomplish rather than making assumptions about their inability to execute particular jobs.

Working with a caregiver on repetitious tasks may be quite fulfilling, as can stacking papers or sorting coins, emptying the dishwasher, and sorting coins.

Organize all of your items into sets to help you decide what to wear. This enables the dementia patient to make wise decisions and maintain some degree of independence.

✳ When someone wants to assist you, try to be kind and accept his assistance. Continually modify the assignment to make him feel helpful. Work side by side with the individual, especially on things he would find challenging to do on his own. This might be difficult at times since working together could need more patience than you have and result in a job taking twice as long.

✳ Establish regular periods for eating, playing games, interacting with others, and silent contemplation.

✳ Post a daily calendar of events in a visible location to serve as a reminder of what has to be done or what is scheduled for the day.

✳ Give the Alzheimer's patient a large monthly calendar so they can keep track of their appointments, travel plans, and special events. Some people constantly wonder when forthcoming events will occur because they are anxious about them.

✳ To remind people when their medications are due, use medicine holders with timers. Alternately, make it a habit to dispense the medications at the same time each day. Carry the dosages in little medication cases if you will be out together at one of the times. It is simple and discrete to administer the medication.

✳ Try to be as adaptable as you can to the dementia patient's shifting moods. Avoid rigid timetables at all costs.

✳ Find strategies to change the surroundings to suit the person's evolving demands. Use soap on a rope to make it less likely that someone may slip and fall in the shower or tub while using the soap. Invest in equipment that switch themselves off after a brief period of use, such as electric coffee makers, teapots, and irons.

Consider the following advice as well. Respect the need for sociability and provide for it:

✳ Make plans for a senior companion or friend to visit once a week, and to accompany the Alzheimer's patient to the movies, the zoo, or the mall. ✳ Keep including people who have Alzheimer's disease in the social activities that they took part in before developing the illness. Due of the work required, this might be challenging at times. However, interacting with people improves one's attitude, may be relieving, and can lead to pleasant surprises.

✳ Be mindful that people with Alzheimer's disease become increasingly reliant on their main caregiver and may get upset if they are separated from them. The individual with Alzheimer's disease may often "shadow" the caretaker, denying the latter any opportunity for alone.

✳ Decide on some boundaries for your privacy, your time alone, or your quiet periods, such when you're working on your computer, cooking dinner, or reading a book. The individual with Alzheimer's disease will often respect these quiet moments if they are tenderly but forcefully safeguarded.

✳ Keep in mind that although maintaining good personal cleanliness and dressing correctly is crucial for an adult who is able to function normally, it often progressively loses significance in the life of a person with Alzheimer's disease. Even if he increasingly need help with all facets of personal care, it might sometimes still be crucial. A person's dignity, self-respect, and wellbeing are all enhanced by being well-groomed and clothed. The caregiver also feels better because of it.

✳ Keep in mind that the person with Alzheimer's disease may participate in creating the legal and financial papers necessary to handle future demands early in the course of the illness.

People who have Alzheimer's disease often accept that they have the condition and begin making plans for long-term care.

✳ As a caretaker, keep an eye on yourself to make sure you're not putting up barriers and living in denial. Help people with Alzheimer's disease finish the paperwork they need to, and don't take away their chance to do so when they're ready.

✳ Be receptive to inquiries or discussions about the causes of the changes. The individual might ponder "Why is this happening to me?" as he emerges from denial.

✳ Assist the Alzheimer's patient in reflecting on her own abilities, both easy and difficult.

✳ By saying something such, "You seem sad," you may assist the person with Alzheimer's disease in labeling their emotions. "Are you finding this frustrating?" "You are now experiencing anger. You are aware that anger is acceptable.

✳ Try to comprehend the reasons behind certain challenging actions. What are a few of the things that are causing the behavior? What are the elements that are under your control?

It is critical to **try** to identify factors contributing to the issue, whether they are environmental, medical, or communication related.

.✳ To assist the individual with Alzheimer's disease preserve his skills as long as possible or to make up for decreases, schedule frequent vision and hearing exams. A person's capacity for understanding might be impacted by issues with their vision or hearing.

The majority of the time, a person with early-to-mild Alzheimer's disease is fully mobile. As long as possible, let the individual enjoy their freedom. Encourage safe walking and exercise.

Keep them engaged

✳ Be aware that ambulation issues develop gradually and fluctuate depending on the circumstances. For instance, it can be confusing to move a few steps forward while in line before stopping. You may need to gently persuade the individual to go on. Avoid walking on shiny surfaces because these can make people with dementia feel icy or slippery. ✳ The person with Alzheimer's disease may get terrified by all the activity and hesitate to leave a busy area, which makes it difficult. ✳ Walking into a shop or other facility might become slower and getting out of automobiles can take more time. It is useless to urge someone who has Alzheimer's to "hurry up."

✳ If someone is reluctant to go on solitary walks, consider finding alternate means of exercise, such as throwing a ball, dancing, or rhythmic activities (even if he previously thoroughly enjoyed going for long and daily walks).

Consider visiting a mall where the individual may securely stroll beside you. bring two pals with you.

One may stroll beside your loved one, while the other can sit next to you so they can still see you. This gives you a break and gives the person with Alzheimer's disease the exercise they need.

When climbing or descending stairs, keep an eye out for a loss of control. Stumbling might develop into a risky issue. People who suffer from dementing diseases often have a reduction in one or more of these senses.

Activate the senses

✳ If your loved one enjoyed receiving hugs, kisses, or close touches before the start of Alzheimer's disease, keep doing so. Engage in activities that engage the senses, such as cooking, gardening, music, and other creative pursuits.

✳ People might find solace in quiet and in religious rituals.

✳ Say the person's name aloud many times while lightly touching their arm or hand to get their attention. Take cautious not to frighten the individual.

Direct your conversation to the Alzheimer's patient. Refrain from conversing with anyone besides the Alzheimer's patient. It demonstrates a lack of regard for that person's dignity. Especially if the person with Alzheimer's disease sits quietly, this is not always simple to do. Sadly, it is possible to lose track of him. Increase visual appeal by paying attention to lighting, employing colors, and creating visual contrasts between the walls and the flooring. Concentration levels may be impacted by inadequate lighting.

✳ Make sure your home is adequately lit by checking each room. Brighter lightbulbs should be used instead of low-wattage ones. This is especially useful in the winter when the sun might not be as bright.

✳ Check the lighting outside. It's very helpful to have light sensors that illuminate when someone approaches your house.

✳ Be cautious of tile floors with patterns that resemble steps because they can throw people off balance. A highly polished surface or strong sunlight glare might also be problematic.

✳ Play music that will energize, thrill, or relax the individual who has Alzheimer's.

✳ Three or four times a week, set the table with flowers and cook a dish you know they'll like. This use of the senses improves the quality of life for both you and the dementia patient.

CHAPTER 3

The Average/Moderate Stage: A Lot Happening Simultaneously

Second Typical Scene

Alexander's Delight is a favorite restaurant of your father and you, therefore the two of you have made plans to lunch there. He is 86 years old today.

You knock on the door and request a special table that has been set aside towards the wall and at the rear of the room. There will be a bit more quiet there. It is your father's 86th birthday today, so you inform the waiter when you ask for your reserved table. "You don't have to let everyone know that it's my birthday", according to your father. "I'm not really aging. Just keep it quiet for now".

To take your orders, the waiter arrives. Give me a hamburger and some spiders, requests your father. The waiter apologizes after glancing at your father. What exactlydid you say? I want a hamburger and some spiders, your dad says. "Dad will have the hamburger and French fries", you remark as you intervene. The waiter nods in agreement while finishing the order. Your dad's actions have been evolving. When he goes out in public, he feels more uneasy and does not have the same amount of energy as previously. He still understands what he wants, but he can no longer put it into words.

Your deepest awareness can be that life isn't turning out the way you had imagined it would for you and your loved one. So many skills seem to have vanished. But so many still do. A caregiver might get tips on how to make the life of the person with Alzheimer's disease happier and more comfortable by concentrating on what is still there.

Remind yourself that the sickness is gaining control and that the changes you are seeing in the person for whom you are caring are not deliberate or intentional. Thoughts about oneself are there throughout the illness, they come and go rapidly. Think of Alzheimer's like a slice of Swiss cheese, a nurse said. When things are clear, a person can see through the cracks, but when they're foggy, they struggle to comprehend or think clearly.

The brain's parietal lobes begin to experience damage when Alzheimer's disease advances to the moderate stage. When this happens, the individual is unable to combine information from the senses of sight, hearing, and touch.

✳ Despite the losses, several talents, including judgment, social skills, and the capacity to do certain complicated activities, are still present in the Moderate stage of Alzheimer's disease. Maintaining these and the other functions should be the primary concern of the caregiver.

✳ At this point, the person has problems getting dressed, is confused or lost, and is unable to utilize items.

✳ Since the speech parts of the temporal lobe have already been severely damaged by Alzheimer's disease's destructive process, the individual typically also has a lot of trouble asking for items (or for help).

✳ Driving might be challenging at this stage of the illness since response time is often slowed down no way for the body to coordinate the appropriate bodily reaction for the foot pedals and steering wheel with the whole amount of visual and acoustic information in the surroundings. Patients often see doctors for an evaluation at this time.

Family members and friends become aware that there are issues needing medical assessment when the parietal lobes are affected by this damaging process.

✳ Even if you wish your loved one had total control over her life, you see that more and more circumstances need your active involvement.

✳ At this point, the individual could exhibit behavioral issues including roaming and agitation, in which case additional close monitoring is required.

Try to identify the significance of an inappropriate conduct when you see it. Consider what the other person is attempting to say or accomplish. Later in the day or in the early evening, agitated behaviors often become worse.

✳ As a caregiver, particularly as a husband, you could lose your temper, spout crude remarks, and aid reluctantly. It's crucial to explain to the Alzheimer's patient why you're irritable (usually from not getting enough sleep) and why you say hurtful things.

Keeping the lines of communication open and moving forward cautiously also helps. You can experience conflict at this stage of the illness as you try to balance your needs with those of the person you are caring for.

✳ Especially when changes and transitions in living arrangements are required, be prepared for your own denial as well as the denial stated by your loved one or other family members.

✳ Learn coping mechanisms for your own rage and wounded feelings and ask for assistance from others if you find it difficult to remain impartial in a scenario. The person suffering from dementia may sometimes get enraged and accuse her partner or children of doing something they haven't done. Unintentionally making offensive statements is possible.

✳ Think about how you handle the individual who has Alzheimer's. If the conversation becomes hostile, consider the following: "Am I in any danger?" "Am I able to handle this?"

Frequently, just five steps back and separating yourself from the individual for a little period of time can prevent injury. On the other hand, you must be more forceful to protect the individual if he is about to leave the home and enter a busy street.

✳ Use other resources and depend on professionals. As your loved one enters the next phase of the illness, assigning responsibilities to others can help you maintain the strength and energy that will be required.

✳ Consider holding family forums where you may inform family members on the previous financial and emergency plans that have been established. If such preparations have not been made, make them right away. Plan and notify your family of your plans.

✳ Don't let everyday stress and disappointments drive you to snappy responses.

✳ When you discover that you need a break or have lost your balance or attention, remove yourself from the caring environment. Your loved one's long-term memory could still be intact even if their short-term memory may have vanished. The caregiver may benefit from this advice.

Encourage Memory

✳ Accept without reservation the possibility that the person for whom you are caring may forget daily or hourly details such as what is on the schedule, any travel arrangements, and the whereabouts of everyday items like dishes, pans, and silverware. Plans may need to be repeated regularly.

✳ Make time to pause and think about life. Look through old picture albums and recall fun and joyful occasions.

✳ Play the game of beanbags. Place two seats facing one another, approximately 5 or 6 feet apart. The individual with Alzheimer's disease sits on one chair while the carer occupies the other.

A basic inquiry that may be answered in one or two words is posed to the Alzheimer's patient while the caregiver simultaneously throws the bean bag.

The procedure is then repeated while tossing the beanbag back to the caregiver. Invite the individual with Alzheimer's disease to the game to change things up. to pose a query to the caregiver. Sing well-known tunes that stir up sentimental recollections.

✳ To assist the individual recall knowledge that came so easily in the past, label plants, items, and drawers. More freedom is possible for the individual if they can name items. Use easy-to-read labels that are big and bold. Accept the memories that are still there: When the person for whom they are caring can no longer follow even the most basic instructions, it may frighten and disturb a caregiver. This doesn't always develop gradually. You realize all of a sudden that even if you say something as straightforward as, "Put this out in the trash," he will not grasp what you mean and will not be able to follow your instructions. It's reasonable to feel truly frustrated after this defeat.

You won't find yourself handling this loss more creatively until you progressively comprehend the implications of it.

Continue delivering instructions. Just keep in mind that if he has short-term memory loss, you may need to assist him or omit any of the stages from the work. Simple chores are best.

While you should be honest in telling the person who has Alzheimer's disease that she has a memory problem, doing so will only make her feel less worthy of respect and self-esteem.

Try to reassure the individual of her continued worth and how much she can still accomplish.

Try To Comprehend Their Language

Be warned that some individuals with Alzheimer's disease may use the incorrect term in a statement at this point.

Instead of saying, "I want to comb my hair," the individual would say, "I want to eat my hair." Don't make a huge issue out of correcting him; just demonstrate that you understand. As the dementia worsens, use these suggestions to help the patient. Create a welcoming atmosphere

✳ Even if the individual keeps telling the same tale, let them tell stories.

✳ Avoid using phrases like "shake a leg" or "jump into bed" that might be misconstrued.

✳ Never quarrel with a dementia sufferer. He won't do anything except become angrier, more perplexed, and annoyed. Ask yourself whether the argument you are making is indeed a life or death matter. Is there a dispute about entering a major roadway at rush hour? If so, you must consider the necessity for safety. But if the argument is about whether he is wearing black or blue trousers, save your time and effort.

✳ When someone cries out, "It's so hard!" or "I don't know what's going on!" or "I don't know what to do!" listen carefully and sympathize with their perplexity. If you can, share a joke about how absurd life can be.

✳ When speaking with the person who has dementia, make every effort to be at eye level.

✳ Avoid using complicated language since people with dementia may have problems comprehending it; instead, use short, basic words that explain one major concept. Allow plenty of time for the information to sink in between phrases.

✳ Always face the individual while speaking to her and approach carefully. Be mindful of your facial expressions since, particularly if you are annoyed by her actions, she could infer your emotions from them.

✳ To keep the person with dementia from being distracted and hearing confusing signals, try to reduce background noise and have conversations in calm areas. ✳ Give the person with dementia as much time as necessary to reply to questions, requests, or verbal sharing. As soon as the knowledge is completely understood, it might turn into a tiresome guessing game. Despite the challenges, it's crucial to keep the lines of communication open.

✳ Try humour and cheerfulness; a non-demanding attitude can frequently assist carers get through challenging times. If you can turn it into a joke or fun, getting someone to get out of bed or to the restroom is often simpler.

✳ Gaining someone's trust comes first. This often makes a work much easier. Spending some time speaking before beginning the activity at hand is one method to do this. To assist the individual to relax, spend some time chatting about the weather, family members, or another consoling subject.

✳ Remember that people lose their capacity to interpret language as their impairments worsen. So, instead of saying, "It's time for lunch," you may need to add, "Here is your soup at this table." Additionally, they could use phrases from their youth or earlier in life, making it harder to understand questions like "Do you need to go to the bathroom?" or "Do you need to urinate?"

✳ Speak in a friendly, relaxed way. Try to speak in the way you would want to be addressed.

✳ Maintain a low vocal pitch. Sometimes there is a temptation to yell when someone doesn't instantly grasp. Simply said, this will agitate the dementia patient and make communication more challenging.

✳ If a dementia patient starts to grow agitated, try redirecting her by switching to another activity or topic of discussion to take her mind off the agitating factor. Find out what is causing the agitation. Change occurs every day due to the disease's unrelenting progression. Caretakers need to be vigilant at all times and have the ability to accept that what worked yesterday may not work today.

In the face of ongoing change, reevaluating alternatives and developing fresh strategies are all part of the challenging task that is caring. Sometimes a caregiver may ask a person with dementia to do an activity that, although seeming easy to the caregiver, is quite challenging to the person with Alzheimer's disease.

Due of the many stages required, chores like getting dressed or brushing your teeth are examples of those that are exceedingly complicated. Let the individual with Alzheimer's disease take care of as much of themselves as they can.

Learn To Simplify Things

✳ To ensure that someone can continue to complete a work effectively, break it down into manageable, tangible stages. Verify that the individual is taking one modest step at a time. Occasionally, caregivers may combine numerous actions without recognizing the patient may no longer be able to do two or three steps at once.

✳ Always give yourself enough time to prepare for an outing or to get dressed. It's crucial to avoid rushing a dementia patient since this might agitate them.

✳ Wear easy-to-care-for clothes, such as slippers with Velcro closures or tube socks that can't be worn backwards. To make dressing easier, choose garments with front closures or Velcro fasteners.

✳ Try to concentrate on the routine activities that the individual performed before to the commencement of the disease, such as making beds, folding clothes, gardening, and washing and drying dishes.

Dementia patients eventually lose the capacity to pick up new skills or jobs.

Change The Surroundings

Maintain a backup pair of dentures, and occasionally ensure that they fit comfortably. If required, install a childproof lock on the cabinet drawers and refrigerator. Instead of stairs, think about using a ramp with railings. For safety purposes, remove the stove's knobs.

Check garbage cans before emptying them since a demented person could have thrown away something priceless. When not in use, remove the fuel sources from grills and patio equipment. Remove throw rugs and scatter rugs to reduce the risk of slipping and falling.

Remove the trash cans from the bathrooms and bedrooms since a dementia patient can mistake them for a toilet.

✳ Store cleaning and laundry supplies in a secured cabinet.

✳ Keep drugs out of children's reach and establish a morning and nightly schedule for distributing them.

✳ Encourage the patient to drink an 8- to 10-ounce glass of cold water every time she takes a tablet. She may first not want to drink the whole glass, but if you gently insist on her finishing it, she will eventually become accustomed to doing so.

✳ Check to see whether the individual has trouble swallowing. If so, get his doctor to evaluate him.

✳ Always keep your safety in mind. Does the individual have to sit to dress or take a bath? The person's ability to shave safely?

✳ Consider the ideal time of day for family reunions. Evening visits are preferred to daytime activities. Consider include the person with Alzheimer's disease when planning special events to preserve the feeling of the family as a unit.

✳ Any memory, behaviour, or personality changes in your loved one should be brought to the attention of family and friends.

You could wish to recommend suitable dates to visit, as well as suitable activities like a car trip or presents the loved one would like.

Encourage relatives and friends to come over, even if it is difficult for them to do so.

✳ During the appointment, try to limit distractions. Smaller groups of individuals are preferred than larger ones.

✳ Keep in mind that individuals with dementia suffer from memory loss and may get upset or irritated if you ask them questions they are unable to respond to.

Choose a companion who the individual feels comfortable with and in whom you have faith. Inform your loved one of your destination and expected time of absence. You might also bring your mobile phone and use it to contact him to let him know you are returning.

Encourage loved ones to give the dementia patient a regular, planned phone call. Shorten conversations and focus on the subject's likely recall of recent past occurrences.

After the call, engage her in conversation to keep her mind active. You might provide her with a photo of the caller and explain your connection.

✳ Give the Alzheimer's patient suitable presents. Favorite meals, pill crushers, audiobooks, gift cards to a hair salon or for a manicure, as well as homemade certificates good for a drive or a stroll, are a few ideas.

✳ By providing tickets to a concert, a play, a sporting event, or the circus, you may promote socializing.

Make Changes For Eating

✳ Place several pieces of fresh fruit on the table if you are having sandwiches for lunch at home. To eat the fruit with or after the sandwiches, invite the person suffering from Alzheimer's disease to join you.

✳ When going out, assist the individual with Alzheimer's disease in selecting an entree. Because the individual may initially be resistant to assistance, it may need patience on the side of the caregiver.

The best strategy is to gently point to several foods, read aloud the descriptions, and alternate between options until she is happy with her selection. There is no need to rush the procedure, even if you are eating with other people. People are so sweet when they see it, it's fantastic.

When selecting, let the waiter or waitress know which option your loved one prefers. Half-fill glasses with liquid.

It could be required to wrap utensils with foam rubber to improve the grip for someone with demen tia.

Use a pie plate or other dish with a lip to serve food. As a result, it will be simpler to transfer the meal to a spoon or fork, and it won't slip off the plate.

✳ Keep finger foods on hand and visible for convenient snacking. Make sure the food is wholesome and is cut up into bite-sized pieces. The sight of these things will prompt the person with Alzheimer's disease to eat even if they may not express their hunger while they are there.

Reasoning And Judgment Control

As the caretaker of someone with moderate Alzheimer's disease, be aware of your degree of irritability. More carers than they realize struggle with this. Because daily conditions are so unpredictable, anger is a feeling that caregivers experience all too often. Give your loved one confidence.

✳ Be aware that your loved one may not be making the best decisions when it comes to safety.

✳ Accept the anxieties and concerns that people with dementia voice. Recognize earlier conversations and reassure them that you would assist them with their issues.

✳ Support them as they experience any independence loss. Discuss your worries with them and reaffirm your affection for them.

✳ If certain TV shows make you confused, cut down on your watching. Alzheimer's patients could believe that what they see on the screen is really occurring.

✳ If the physical area is just too complicated for the person with dementia, try partitioning off a portion of the home. Try getting rid of any outdated furniture. If the environment is overly cluttered, remove the items.

✳ Make sure that the walking spaces are well-lit and clutter-free.

✳ Give the individual a secure location to stroll in. Make a trail through the home if a person has a tendency to wander. Chairs should be spaced apart to allow for relaxing.

Throw rugs that might trip someone up should be removed. If possible, make the atmosphere simpler to prevent the confused individual from being too overwhelmed.

✳ Every time you want to go from one room to another, ask permission beforehand. Start out by saying something like, "We need to get up immediately." Don't merely drag or push the individual from place to place; instead, gently aid them in getting up from the chair or moving about the room.

✳ Offer guidelines and organization. Instead of asking someone whether they want to do anything, say, "It's time to..." In order to prevent overnight stays, try to plan hospitalizations. It is preferable to bring the guy home with you and have help there than to have him remain somewhere else. Bring comforting objects with you, such as a blanket, photographs, favorite music, or a favorite book, if an overnight stay is required. By doing this, you may increase the person's comfort and lessen their irritation.

✳ When traveling, try to avoid going somewhere unfamiliar. Keep your vacations simple, slow paced, and think about taking several short trips rather than one long trip to help with the super vision of your loved one.

✳ Timetables should be flexible. Give the individual adequate time to prepare. Give the individual time to acclimate to any changes in the timetable. Travel during less-frequented periods of the day.

✳ Keep a list of contacts in case something happens to you on your person, along with information explaining that you are traveling with a person who has dementia. Always keep identification on your loved one.

✳ Enrol your loved one in the Safe Return Program by getting in touch with the Alzheimer's Association. Put on a medical alert identification bracelet for her. Some chapters are able to provide these medical alert IDs without cost thanks to funding. Think about purchasing a medical alert bracelet for yourself.

✳ Bring along materials like comforting images, cassettes, novels, or easy activities to occupy the individual if she starts to become anxious during the trip.

✳ When traveling or attending appointments, allow extra time for bathroom breaks. You may wish to send a companion who is the same sex as the dementia sufferer with them to help out in the bathroom if they are the opposite sex to the caregiver.

✳ Purchase a chair-bound or handicapped person's fitness DVD, and motivate him to keep working out.

People with dementia still have senses including hearing, taste, smell, sight, and touch, as well as memory, judgment, and the capacity to learn new activities. The ability to hear and see may be compromised. Put your attention on the healthy senses to keep dementia sufferers happy.

Enliven The Senses

✳ Even when your words are no longer comprehended, touch your loved one often to express your concern. While some individuals dislike being touched, the majority find a soft touch comforting.

✳ Ensure that your loved one doesn't get dehydrated. Due to their diminished ability to identify their thirst or their tendency to forget to drink, many people with dementia do not consume enough fluids. Dehydration symptoms include lightheadedness, dry skin, flushing, fever, fast heartbeat, disorientation, and an unwillingness to drink.

✳ Maintain a peaceful atmosphere. Dementia sufferers struggle to handle the strain of a bustling atmosphere. When there is too much going on in the surroundings, such as music playing during a discussion or a throng of people, Dementia patients can react indignantly or irritably. Consider if it is too loud or whether the gathering was too big while trying to interpret your loved one's expression of rage or frustration.

✴ Maintain comedy and laughter in your relationship. A resource is daily news print cartoons and stories about family and friends. To the person you are caring for, read aloud books and other items.

✴ Keep in mind the delight that a live animal or bird may provide. Numerous assisted-living homes provide pet therapy services or keep their own animals or birds to foster warm connections.

Invite a family minister, priest, rabbi, or other spiritual advisor to get in touch with the ill individual.

✴ Be mindful that some individuals in this period may reach out to touch everything they see and may inadvertently put objects in their mouths. This could provide a safety risk. Consider the surroundings like you would while child-proofing a home. Remove everything that can be harmful or ingestible.

CHAPTER 4

Advanced/Severe Stage: Making Every Second Worth It.

Third Typical Scene

Alexander's Delight is a favourite restaurant of your father and you, therefore the two of you have made plans to lunch there. He turned 90 years old today. Although he has relocated from his house to an assisted living facility, his Alzheimer's disease has advanced to the point that he will soon need to transfer to a nursing home where he can get more specialized care.

Your dad still enjoys going on rides and sometimes getting ice cream. You want to make it particularly memorable for him since it is his 90th birthday. You make the choice to visit Alexander's Delight with him once again.

You have requested a specific table in a discreet area of the restaurant since your dad is now using a wheelchair. To take your orders, the waiter has arrived. You want your dad to choose an item that will be simple for him to swallow since he has been experiencing some difficulty swallowing. "Dad, what do you want to order?" you enquire. You place an order, he says. You place the order and strike up a chat with your father.

He feels upset as he watches people enter and exit the eatery, which is more noisy than normal. It is preferable, as you can see, to revoke your order and go. You buy your dad ice cream in a Dairy Queen drive-through.

 He is pleased while you ride a short distance. In the severe stage, there is a reduction in one's ability to handle anything challenging. Other body processes often deteriorate and fail. It's crucial to be clean and comfortable.

Giving loved ones the respect and dignity, they deserve is the main objective for carers and family members. People who live and work with people who have the severe form of the condition must be able to "read" body language and pay close attention to any verbal cues in order to fulfill the needs of their loved ones. Time and patience are needed for this technique. Family members and caregivers must take their time and concentrate.

When the frontal lobes get severely damaged, appropriate social interaction becomes impossible. Many people can no longer be cared for at home by carers at this point.

At this point, they have lost a lot of their "civilized" conduct and are losing their social skills, judgment, and ability to think. They react improperly and in an unacceptable way. Caregivers might concentrate on maintaining the residual functions rather than focusing on what is lacking. The individual might exhibit violent outbursts at different points throughout the frontal lobe stage or they can become passive, apathetic, and immobilized.

Helping someone undress, for example, might result in aggression to reject the touch, potentially harming either the caretaker or the target. In its latter stages, Alzheimer's disease kills virtually all of the brain's nerve cells, with the exception of the motor cortex and the visual cortex, which explains why walking and pacing appear to be residents' principal activities in nursing homes.

Even these brain regions are lost in the later stages, leaving the person immobile and mostly unresponsive.

Start To speak With Authority

✻ The majority of decisions pertaining to the wellbeing of the person you are caring for should be made by you. To be able to adapt to the quickly changing demands of the person with Alzheimer's disease, you will need to maintain a good level of health and vitality for yourself.

✻ Both the caregiver and the Alzheimer's patient find it aggravating how difficult it is to communicate. As a caregiver, it is crucial that you be in constant communication with your loved one about things like the food, the weather, the location, someone you were with, upcoming activities like medical visits, social engagements, or the news. Put your attention on techniques to keep the individual informed of what is happening.

✳ You can be dealing with money matters, finding alternate homes, and insurance concerns during this last stage. Ideally, you and the person with Alzheimer's have already spoken about end-of-life matters. Accepting the truth that your loved one no longer acknowledges you could be challenging.

When helping a person with Alzheimer's disease who is in the severe stages, the caregiver should keep the following in mind:

Seizing Every Opportunity Counts

Even if the individual with dementia doesn't reply, talk to him slowly and deliberately. Your voice may provide solace. Pay close attention to treating the patient with respect. Despite the body losing control of some processes, pay attention to your clothing and surroundings.

✳ Spend time listening. Keep in mind that the person you are caring for has the power to accept or reject the food, support, or comfort you wish to provide. Cleanliness, the person's safety requirements, and listening and observing to ascertain the loved one's wants are all within the responsibility of the caregiver.

✳ Inform the medical professionals about the patient's skills and routines. If possible, make hospitalizations in advance to prevent overnight stays. It would be preferable to bring the individual home and provide in-home care rather than having them remain in a strange location.

Bring comforting objects with you if a stay is required, such as a blanket, photographs, favourite music, or a favourite book. This lessens the potential of irritation and makes everyone feel more at ease.

✳ Think about receiving hospice care. Hospice care may be given anywhere: at home, at a nursing home, or in a place of residence like a hospice house.

✳ Spend some time with the patient who is getting healthcare. Any gesture that communicates your presence should be used, such as holding the person's hand, kissing her on the face, rubbing or patting her hand.

✳ Be ready to cope with the possibility that an individual with Alzheimer's disease may have periods of lucidity that come and go. He may not recognize you or could refer to you by a different name. His response will vary.

You'll be able to adapt to the situation better if you're ready for it. Communication will be quite challenging at this point, making it difficult to gauge how much understanding is still there.

Even if she doesn't answer, never assume that the individual doesn't grasp your words of solace and confidence. The individual could recognize words or gestures. Caregivers should explore for novel methods to engage all five senses in conversation.

Interpret nonverbal cues: Accept and anticipate that communication will be limited to a few words or gestures. Pay attention to nonverbal cues like tightening the lips to reject food or tugging at garments to indicate discomfort or concern. A person with Alzheimer's disease in its severe stage may spend most of the time in bed. The person's capacity for difficult jobs has diminished, and they now largely rely on others to take care of them. reduce anxiety and stress: Remove or cover locks with tape, particularly in the bathroom, to prevent dementia patients from locking themselves out. Alternatively, you may take the doors off and provide seclusion with drapes.

✳ Keep in mind the person's requirements while taking a bath. Because the person with dementia may have developed a dread of water, taking a bath may be quite challenging. If at all feasible, the caregiver should join the individual in the shower.

Additionally, a bath or shower chair in a tub may be utilized to reduce water phobia. The individual may be washed with the aid of flexible hand-held shower nozzles.

This will prevent going into the bathtub, which may sometimes result in excessive agitation. Additionally, sit on a shower chair. ✳ For the individual with dementia, prepare to unwrap presents before explaining and demonstrating the purpose of each. Encourage any remaining talents as much freedom as you can.

Put Aside Your Expectations

Give the person with dementia more time to eat since it will take them longer to finish a meal. Consider holidays as a fresh experience. Start new customs that use the person's residual abilities in family gathering events. This is particularly useful if the Alzheimer's patient is no longer able to take part in customary activities during family gatherings.

✳ If decorating or buying presents is too tough for you, enlist the aid of a friend.

✳ Tell your relatives and friends that you need to speak about your loved one since they could be hesitant to bring her up out of concern for your feelings. Be creative with your sadness and share tales with the rest of the family.

✳ Create reasonable expectations. Recognize that the holidays could be challenging and make plans appropriately. Establish boundaries for what you can and cannot accomplish. Are you acting in accordance with your desires or what you believe other people want you to do?

Keep in mind that it is crucial to look after oneself at this point in the caregiving process. Save your energy to maintain your equilibrium so you may appreciate the other loving people in your life.

✳ Keep your emergency contact information visible in your vehicle, in your pocket or handbag, and on your person always.

✳ Always have a mobile phone with you in case of an emergency.

✳ Be mindful of their body's demands. If the individual begins to undress or tugs at clothing, assume that they are too hot or in discomfort and are unable to communicate their desire to go to the bathroom or bed. If someone is acting strangely with their genitalia, do not overreact, become upset, or make fun of them. Try to evaluate the circumstances. Maybe they need to go to the bathroom, or maybe their clothing are too small. Perhaps the individual wants to go to bed but finds it difficult to express this. Redirect the person's activity slowly. Seek outside assistance if sexual troubles persist.

✳ When behaviours like fondling, grasping a woman's breast, or pursuing sexual intimacy happen, gently reroute the individual. If gentle redirection is not an option, look for outside assistance.

✳ If the individual grows irritated when you attempt to convince her to stop the behaviour, try to divert her with another activity, maybe in a nearby room.

✳ When incontinence begins, get the required supplies, such as mattress protectors, flannel-coated rubber pads, and other supplies offered by your pharmacy.

Inactivity might result in skin deterioration and pressure sores. Now is the moment to concentrate on the person's abilities and interests.

Be Inventive

✳ If falling out of bed is a risk, put the mattress and springs of the bed on the floor to protect the dementia patient from harm. Additionally, this may reduce roaming. Place the bedridden person next to a window so they may enjoy the view of the outside. Try to satisfy the person's need to be outside, even if it means moving her bed onto a patio.

✳ If circulation is weak, have comfortable lap robes, warm socks, and blankets on hand to provide comfort.

✳ Learn how to posture the immobile person properly to avoid skin deterioration.

✳ For further suggestions on how to encourage mobility for the person you are caring for, speak with hospice staff. It is now challenging for a caregiver to "read" body language.

Your voice or touch may reassure the individual and let them know you are there. use the senses to convey: Make any permissible contact with the individual, such as combing his hair or softly massaging his arm or chest. Massaging the person's hands, feet, and arms using hand and body lotion. Be aware of any scents that may not be appealing to the individual and stay away from such scented things.

Encourage regular visits from anybody who can help the individual feel less lonely. Giving people with dementia at this stage cute stuffed animals, and plush cushions to stimulate touch might comfort them.

Provide soothing music or noises to the individual. Provide drinks, malts, or anything appropriate with the person's diet and swallowing ability for her to enjoy, even if he may not be able to talk.

There can still be a sugary flavour that you like. When a person with Alzheimer's disease is unable to swallow or suck on a straw, provide liquids using an oral syringe. Use visually beautiful colours, images, and noises to create a comfortable living space. Provide for the person's spiritual need.

CHAPTER 5

Important Information And Answers On Alzheimer

Remember that the goal of this chapter is to assist people with Alzheimer's disease in realizing their dreams and leading happy, fulfilling lives. As a result, caregivers, family members, and friends will get new experiences and learn how to maintain balance in their own lives as they discover new avenues for leading happy, fulfilling lives.

Once an Alzheimer's disease diagnosis has been established by a medical professional and when you feel safe doing so, inform people that you or a loved one has the condition. Unfortunately, much as with cancer, AIDS, and many other illnesses, there is a stigma associated with Alzheimer's disease in our culture.

Some individuals are unwilling to admit that they have the illness, and their families have decided that nobody would discuss it. The Alzheimer's patient and his family may feel embarrassed as a result. Nobody is to blame for developing Alzheimer's disease, and neither the individual who has it nor his or her family should feel embarrassed. Alzheimer's disease is still not completely understood by medical research.

There is currently no treatment for the illness. Still, a conclusive diagnosis can only be made after death. Everyone wants as much control over their life as possible, and accepting the diagnosis enables a person with Alzheimer's disease and her family to engage in preparing for the future.

By educating others about the condition, one may get assistance from local offices of the Alzheimer's Association, state offices on aging, and many other people who have firsthand knowledge of the condition. Many ages may be used to diagnose Alzheimer's disease.

Everyone concerned finds comfort in acknowledging the condition and making plans for the future, which also reassures those who are afflicted that their wishes for their life will be honoured. Twenty-six individuals recently convened during their lunch break at a workshop to exchange knowledge and gain insight into the best ways to care for a person who has just received an Alzheimer's disease diagnosis.

How can I aid my loved one who lives in another state? was a worry shared by more than half of the attendees. Many folks sobbed as they described how they were too far away to often visit their loved ones due to their worry and grief for the distant person. If one doesn't keep a tight check on the person with Alzheimer's disease and their wellbeing, issues may slip overlooked.

Getting in contact with the patient's doctor may be useful in determining if any of these medical or psychological changes warrant concern. You may often check in with the person's doctor if you are far away.

You may still be there for any significant transitional changes that will take place in your loved one's life with the doctor's assistance. Most attendees at the class were unaware that there are regional branches of the Alzheimer's Association all around the country.

Your efforts in the caregiving process may be aided by contact with these organizations. You will then have another person to aid you in addition to the doctor. You may assist a loved one with legal and financial issues even from a distance.

Choosing the finest care for a loved one who has Alzheimer's disease is one of the most challenging chores for families. Finding out the loved one's preferences for care throughout the sickness process is the first step. Early in the course of the illness, the loved one should be encouraged to express his desires for a variety of things, including how he would want to be cared for as the sickness advances.

To ensure that friends and family are aware of the loved one's desires, it is crucial to make this choice in the early stages of the illness. This gives the loved one the most amount of power over his life. The greatest method to guarantee that your loved one's wishes are honoured is to use the Family Forum. In some families, these forums are formalized by inviting significant family members to a meeting with an agenda. Other forums happen more randomly since individuals often come together for trips or holidays.

The initial meeting should examine the realities of what occurs as the illness progresses and consider how to carry out the desires of the loved one. While family members want to be able to fulfill all of the deceased person's desires, it is crucial to keep in mind that promises should never be made that may not be maintained.

It is crucial that someone be given the power to carry out the caregiving plans at family meetings. Other family members will undoubtedly help with the caregiving duties, and they can handle other matters like financial planning.

To keep them updated on the loved one's development, the person assigned the task for caring should create a channel of contact with other family members. The obligations may be split up if the individual with Alzheimer's disease has kids.

The loved one's knowledge of how to be cared for is crucial. If there is just one family member, such as a kid or a spouse, that person is responsible for all caregiving duties. She may, however, organize a Family Forum with more family members and friends to incorporate larger groups in the caring arrangements.

When the Alzheimer's patient is alone, a particularly close relative or friend should take the initiative and organize a Family Forum for the person's friends and family. The same procedure is followed: the individual is given the chance to express his preferences for care as the condition progresses, and then it is decided who has the power to act in his best interests.

It's crucial to consider the talents and abilities a person with Alzheimer's disease still has at every stage of the illness. Throughout the course of the illness, there will probably be many family gatherings.

WHAT ARE SOME IMPORTANT FINANCIAL CONSIDERATIONS AS ALZHEIMER'S DISEASE PROGRESSES?

An older senior, an adult child, or a friend is being cared for by around one-fourth of American households. In contrast to the almost equal distribution of men and women who receive care, more than half of carers are female. The average care provider is a married woman in her mid-forties with a household income of $35,000, works full-time, has her high school diploma, and is in her mid-forties.

Between 20% and 40% of caregivers are thought to be members of the "sandwich generation," who are responsible for both an elderly relative and youngsters under the age of 18. Without family caregivers, the long-term care system as it is now would fail. The annual contribution of America's caretakers was projected to be $257 billion in 2004. One in ten Americans said they had a family member with Alzheimer's disease, and one in three said they knew someone who had.

A person with Alzheimer's disease requires a lifetime of care that typically costs $174,000 in total. According to estimates from the Alzheimer's Association and the National Institute on Aging, the yearly cost of caring for people with Alzheimer's disease in the United States exceeds $100 billion.

Up to 7 out of 10 patients with Alzheimer's disease get 75% of their direct care from family and friends at home. An average of $12,500 must be spent annually to cover the remaining 25% of care, which is often covered by family members.

For a person with Alzheimer's disease, a nursing home stay costs $42,000 a year on average. There are also further data on the expense of care for families that have a member who has been diagnosed with Alzheimer's disease. But as the condition progresses, this short analysis demonstrates that caretakers will want support with financial issues. Many people who have the condition think they have saved for the future and will have the money to pay for treatment for the rest of their lives.

Experience has shown that an individual with Alzheimer's disease may swiftly exhaust their funds. When that occurs, the Alzheimer's patient must rely on family resources as well as state and federal aid.

Caregivers should enable a discussion to make plans for the loved one's future care as soon as a family member is given the diagnosis. Due to the importance of discussing the care of the whole person, the family discussion might go a variety of directions.

The following collection of financial papers is provided as a guide to assist you handle the financial assets of a loved one. Even if you believe you are already acquainted with these materials, review them nevertheless and start making the required preparations. Information about your bank and brokerage accounts; insurance policies; monthly expenses and unpaid debts; stock and bond certificates; Social Security payment details; retirement benefits; unrestricted income; personal property; and mortgage or other ownership documents.

A financial planner may assist you in making plans to satisfy the desires of the individual suffering from Alzheimer's disease while also safeguarding your own family's financial situation.

WHAT ARE SOME IMPORTANT LEGAL QUESTIONS TO TAKE INTO ACCOUNT AS ALZHEIMER'S DISEASE PROGRESSES?

Both legal and economical concerns are taken into consideration throughout the planning phase. Elder law, which deals with issues including guardianship determination, spousal impoverishment, disability planning, living wills or trusts, and durable powers of attorney, is a specialty practice area for many attorneys. The capacity required to take part in the preparation and execution of the documents may also be ascertained with the aid of an attorney.

The Alzheimer's patient needs assistance from the caregiver with the following issues: Make a lasting power of attorney.

This document grants power for financial and/or medical decision-making. It states either that "this power of attorney shall become effective upon the disability or incapacity of the principle" or that "this power of attorney shall not be impacted by the future disability or incapacity of the primary."

If the power of attorney is not "durable," it loses its authority when the Alzheimer's patient loses mental capacity.

Establish a living will. The living will's maker's last desires are outlined in this document. It may be used to describe actions like refusing life-supporting care. In the United States, a living will might take many forms depending on the state.

✳ Organize a will. This paper outlines what ought to happen to a person's assets and belongings upon death. Consult a specialist for assistance on these issues to help make the process simpler.

✳ Determine who oversees providing care for the dementia patient; always make plans for a backup. To assess le gal capacity, speak with a medical expert. Ascertain if contracts were signed before the Alzheimer's disease diagnosis. Distribute copies of the durable power of attorney to each person listed.

Give copies of your durable power of attorney and living will to your doctor and other healthcare professionals. Make a list of your immediate family, attorneys, financial advisors, and accountants for future use.

Make sure all financial and legal papers are accessible in case of emergency and let others know where they are stored. Taking care of legal and financial matters helps soothe the dementia patient, their family, and other concerned parties.

Everyone can concentrate on the day-to-day care concerns and come up with innovative methods to enhance the dignity of life when there are preparations in place to address the financial and legal requirements of the person with Alzheimer's disease.

WHAT ROLE COULD DRUGS AND OTHER CONDITIONS HAVE IN THE DEVELOPMENT OF ALZHEIMER'S DISEASE?

People with dementia are particularly susceptible to overmedication, drug interactions, and the many negative effects of different medicines.

Medication side effects might include confusion and abrupt changes in a person's level of functioning. Sedatives and tranquilizers used to induce sleep or calm behaviour might impair bladder function and result in incontinence.

The utilization of novel and experimental drugs to treat Alzheimer's disease is the subject of many research investigations conducted all around the globe. The patient with Alzheimer's disease and the carers must weigh the benefits and drawbacks of taking part in such medication studies, including any possible adverse effects.

✳ Confusion may result from or be exacerbated by acute illnesses including a urinary tract infection, pneumonitis, gastrointestinal infection, or any condition that raises the body's temperature. Because they struggle to express symptoms, persons with dementia often have difficulty identifying acute diseases. Any abrupt changes in behaviour should be evaluated with a doctor since they might be signs of an acute disease.

✳ Angina, congestive heart failure, or diabetes are examples of chronic conditions that may impact a person's mood and level of functioning. Additionally, irritation may result from long-term discomfort from headaches, ulcers, or arthritic conditions. ✳ Constipation may be quite unpleasant and may cause behavioural changes. Help the Alzheimer's patient take Metamucil or other stool softeners once or twice a day with a full glass of water in order to maintain regular bowel movements.

✳ Depression's cognitive impairment, memory loss, apathy, and sleep difficulties might resemble dementia. When assessing a patient for Alzheimer's disease or any kind of dementia, it is crucial for the doctor to take the diagnosis of depression into account.

HOW DO YOU KNOW WHEN IT'S TIME TO CHANGE THE PERSON WITH ALZHEIMER'S LIVING CONDITIONS?

When deciding whether to modify the way the Alzheimer's patient lives, a few factors should be taken into account: The patient's mental and physical health; The disease's stage, the main caregiver's general capacity to go on providing care, both the caregiver's and the loved one's financial situation.

Caregiver resources include local offices on aging, the Alzheimer's Association chapters throughout the United States, and medical specialists if an Alzheimer's disease or associated dementia diagnosis has been established.

Obtain information about the illness and the cost of treatment.

HOW IS THE PERSON WITH ALZHEIMER'S DISEASE AFFECTED BY THEIR LIVING CONDITIONS?

"If you've met one Alzheimer's resident, you've met one Alzheimer's resident," goes the proverb. The phrase, which isn't very hilarious, nonetheless puts into perspective what ought to be obvious when considering all facets of the life of the person who has Alzheimer's disease, including the living environment.

It is truly an "individual's" environment, whether it is their house or a shared living space. Fully utilizing the environment possible for people with Alzheimer's disease requires creatively altering it for the individual and changing it as the illness advances.

As a sign of independence, elderly people often drive their cars for much longer than is safe. Being reliant on others is a severe psychological blow that often leads to a decline in physical health. Giving people options is essential to keeping them dependent.

These options might be simple or complicated, depending on the situation. A person's ability to choose what to wear and appropriately dress themselves may make the difference between a good day and a poor day. Food selections improve meal enjoyment and reduce the need for dietary supplements.

Giving someone the freedom to choose their window treatments and bedroom wall colour personalizes their private area and might make it easier for them to recognize it. It may be extremely challenging to maintain privacy in any living arrangement when there are other people around, yet doing so is essential to a person's emotional well-being. Personal mementos should be displayed conspicuously. Changing the items on a regular basis may keep people interested.

Stimulation throughout the environment, from the artwork on the walls, to the style of furniture, to the texture of fabrics, all combine to heighten a per son's sense of emotional security and familiarity with the environment.

To keep someone interested in his surroundings, variation in the environment is crucial. A person's private zone will be less likely to be infiltrated by others if it is noticeable. Exterior areas stimulate the senses and may bring back memories of the warmth of the sun, the sensation of a wind on the skin, or the aroma of flowers.

Every individual has a unique daily and seasonal rhythm that involves eating, sleeping, and using the restroom. Each person's rhythm should be respected, encouraged, and balanced against the caregiver's rhythm, but it should never be changed only for the caregiver's convenience. By removing obstacles to eating, bathing, and using the bathroom while still paying attention to safety concerns, an environment may be designed that accommodates individual rhythms without interfering with the rhythms of others. Paying close attention to even the tiniest details results in a successful workplace.

The setting must respect a person's privacy while preserving security, provide desired company while allowing for seclusion, and give stimulation while still respecting a person's daily routines. Instead of creatively altering the environment to fit the demands of the individual, we should aim to alter it to fulfill those needs so that the environment can improve the quality of life for the person with Alzheimer's disease.

CHAPTER 6

Caring For Yourself Too As A Caregiver

It is now time to focus on your needs—the requirements that you, the caregiver, have as a person as well as in your function as caretaker. In short, I discovered that caretakers want attention as well. What kind of care do most carers require?

To begin, they need information about the sickness they are coping with and its progression; emotional support and appreciation for the many contributions they are making; awareness of community resources, as well as legal and financial assistance.

They must also comprehend the nature of the caretaker position and how to safeguard their own well-being and self-esteem. Try to join a caregiver support group. The leader of such a group should have a thorough awareness of Alzheimer's disease and the role of carers, as well as group counselling abilities. Participation in a support group, according to the majority of carers, not only nourishes them but also has a significant therapeutic impact.

As members of a well-functioning group, students will discover that they may raise any issue that is bothering them without fear of being judged or not being taken seriously.

Even if this is not the case, members of the caregiver group will often figure out a viable solution to that difficulty, as well as any number of other ever-changing challenges that one of its members is experiencing.

Participation in promising clinical research, for example, will spread like wildfire throughout the group. Caregivers who did not have the benefit of belonging to a caregiver group often expressed the feeling that they were losing out on a key lifeline.

To be clear, not all support groups will fulfill the requirements of everyone searching for one. One experienced caregiver suggests that you try more than one group, both to learn from one group and to discover the group that best matches you. Caregiving support groups include men and women, spouses and ex-spouses, sons and daughters, sons-in-law and daughters-in-law, all of whom provide a unique perspective to the caregiver experience.

Manuel was a wealthy businessman, philanthropist, and community activist. He and his wife, Cathy, were inseparable. They travelled everywhere together. At the age of seventy, Cathy started to repeat herself endlessly; she often forgot her keys, missed her check book, and needed to be reminded of upcoming appointments.

Manuel first attempted to excuse Cathy's amnesia and conceal his worry for her from friends and family members. He refused to accept the possibility that she was acquiring Alzheimer's disease. However, when her symptoms worsened, he felt worried enough to seek expert assistance. Cathy was checked, and physicians informed Manuel that she had Alzheimer's disease. Cathy was put on therapy right away. Her doctor recommended Manuel early on to consider obtaining assistance with caring for his wife, but he maintained that he would be the only caregiver. He and Cathy were both extremely private individuals, and neither of them liked the notion of a stranger entering their house.

As Cathy's condition worsened and Manuel had to do more and more for her, he got more unhappy and exhausted, but he refused to accept aid with his caregiving tasks. Cathy was disturbed and woke up numerous times throughout the night, while Manuel slept very little.

Nonetheless, he insisted on doing everything for her and that no one else could care for Cathy as effectively as he could. Within twenty-four hours, two things happened: Cathy awoke in the middle of the night and fell in the bathroom, hurting her chest and head, and Manuel injured his back while attempting to pull her off the bathroom floor. He ultimately phoned his daughter and gave her permission to hire live-in assistance for both of them. A few weeks later, he told Cathy's doctor, "I'm so glad we finally have. The tale of Manuel and Cathy teaches us to share the weight of caring sooner rather than later. This is for both your advantage and the benefit of your loved one. If you can offer more aid while your loved one can still readily create new connections, it will reduce the need to accept further help later in the illness's course.

To offer all the assistance that is required, a team of carers is required. Don't worry; you'll always be the team's leader, but others can help you out. It will enrich your life and the lives of your loved one.

First and foremost, carers are not immune to harm. Without assistance, they may feel disheartened, sad, or burnout, and consequently, they may begin to ignore their own or their patient's care. When a caregiver is completely distraught, he or she may even turn aggressive to their loved ones. You do not want to be one of them. Such effects may be avoided with the support of a caregiver. But there is another reason for meticulous preparation and ensuring that someone else can give part of the necessary care: you may die before your loved one.

You may get in an accident, acquire an unexpected medical ailment, or become a victim of a natural or civil catastrophe. Planning and dividing the load of care helps ensure that your loved one has a safety net in place in the event that anything were to happen to you

During the lengthy months and years when the patient is in the latter stages of the illness, this choice may be extremely suitable and useful. (In the early stages of the condition, the patient may detest attending, maybe because he or she views it as degrading, but in the very late stages, he or she may be unable to engage physically or cognitively.)

Adult day-care programs include a variety of exciting and enjoyable activities such as chatting, remembering, dancing, easy exercises, listening to music or singalongs, and viewing movies. The socializing that occurs in day-care programs with staff and other patients is also very beneficial to the patients. Not to mention, adult day-care offers you, the caregiver, time to yourself during the hours that your loved one attends. Some programs are available five days a week or even on weekends.

Use such hours to attend to your personal needs, such as going to the beauty salon or barbershop, playing golf, going to the doctor, socializing with your friends, attending church, or just having fun. Allow yourself to enjoy life and do whatever will benefit your health and pleasure during these hours.

You will be much more rejuvenated and revitalized when you return to caring. Participating in childcare programs is often inexpensive since these programs are frequently sponsored by public funds, provide a sliding-scale charge structure that takes your financial condition into consideration, or both.

Take a longer break from caregiving: the wedding of an adult child or other relative, a college graduation, a family reunion, or even an elective medical treatment. Thar that you explore enrolling your patient in a respite care program.

A handful of enlightened assisted living facilities or nursing homes with dedicated memory care sections provide care for a week or two, occasionally even up to three weeks. Your loved one will be well cared for while you are gone, and you will both be glad to see each other when you return. Because you may ultimately have to consider putting your loved one in such care, respite care stays may sometimes provide as a sample of the sort of care your patient would get at such a facility.

CONCLUSION

With the progression of the illness, your responsibility for handling everyday duties will grow if you are caring for someone who has Alzheimer's disease or a similar dementia. Consider useful advice that may help you handle chores efficiently while allowing the person with dementia to engage as much as possible.

Lessen irritability

When once-easy chores become challenging, a person with dementia may get irritated. To reduce difficulties and reduce frustration:

Plan your time well. Create a daily schedule. Certain actions, like taking a bath or going to a doctor's visit, are simpler when the individual is most awake and rested. Give yourself some leeway for unplanned events or especially trying days.

Give it some time. Plan additional time for tasks and be prepared for them to take longer than usual. Allow time between jobs for breaks.

Include the individual. Give the dementia patient as little help as possible so that they may do as much as they can. For instance, if you put out clothing in the order they go on, he or she may be able to dress independently or set the table with the use of visual clues.

Give options. Every day, provide a few, but not too many, options. Give them a choice between two clothing, inquire as to whether they prefer a hot or cold beverage, or inquire as to whether they would like to take a stroll or watch a movie.

Give clear directions. Clear, one-step communication is most easily understood by people with dementia.

Put a cap on naps. Avoid taking extended or numerous naps throughout the day. By doing so, the possibility of days and nights switching places is reduced.

lessen the distractions To help the dementia patient concentrate during meals and talks, turn off the TV and reduce other distractions.

Be Adaptable

A dementia patient will gradually become increasingly dependent. Stay adaptable and modify your routine and expectations as necessary to minimize frustration. Consider purchasing a few similar clothes, for instance, if the person wants to wear the same thing every day. If taking a bath is greeted with reluctance, think about doing it less often.

Establish a secure environment

Dementia affects judgment and problem-solving abilities, which raises the risk of damage for a person. To encourage safety

Avoid falling. Prevent falls by avoiding scatter rugs, extension cables, and any other debris. Install grab bars or railings in high-traffic areas.

Apply locks. Install locks on any cabinets that house potentially hazardous items including medicines, alcohol, firearms, poisonous cleaning products, and potentially hazardous utensils and equipment.

Verify the water's temperature. To avoid burns, turn down the hot water heater's thermostat.

Take steps to avoid fires. Keep lighters and matches out of kids' reach. If the dementia patient smokes, always keep an eye on them. A fire extinguisher should be within reach, and smoke and carbon monoxide detectors should have functioning batteries.

Each individual with Alzheimer's disease will have a unique experience with the illness's symptoms and development. Adapt these helpful suggestions to your family member's requirements.

You may overcome the difficulties and annoyances that lie ahead by exercising patience and flexibility, taking care of yourself, and receiving support from friends and family.

www.ingramcontent.com/pod-product-compliance
Lightning Source LLC
Chambersburg PA
CBHW071043250726
48653CB00005B/1978